Music for Score Reading

Robert A. Melcher

Professor of Music Theory
The Conservatory of Music
Oberlin College

Willard F. Warch

Associate Professor of Music Theory
The Conservatory of Music
Oberlin College

PRENTICE-HALL, INC., Englewood Cliffs, New Jersey

64348

Printed in the United States of America
13-607507-X
Library of Congress Catalog Card No.: 78-119859

Current printing (last digit):

10   9   8   6   5   4   3   2

PRENTICE-HALL INTERNATIONAL, INC., London
PRENTICE-HALL OF AUSTRALIA, PTY. LTD., Sydney
PRENTICE-HALL OF CANADA, LTD., Toronto
PRENTICE-HALL OF INDIA PRIVATE LIMITED, New Delhi
PRENTICE-HALL OF JAPAN, INC., Tokyo

CONTENTS

iii

PREFACE

One of the most admired musical accomplishments is performance on the piano of a reasonably faithful version of a full orchestral score. However, it is not the purpose of this book to carry students to the advanced stages of this skill, but rather to develop basic techniques. More importantly, everyone who faithfully studies these lesson assignments, be he an advanced or only elementary pianist, will learn to read music written in the various C clefs and for the transposing instruments of the orchestra and band with the same ease and pleasure that he now reads music written for his own instrument.

Score reading is a complex process that must be developed step by step. This book consists of carefully graded excerpts, beginning with music involving only the treble and bass clefs and progressing through a systematic presentation of the various elements of score reading.

Reading transposing instruments can be done in one of two ways:

1. by interval or transposition, that is, by thinking up or down a certain interval,

2. by clef transposition, that is, by imagining another clef which will give the pitches the instrument sounds, though not always in the correct octave range.

Each system has its advocates, and each system presents its own problems. If the transposition involves only a whole- or half-step, or possibly a third, interval transposition is not difficult. But this thought process becomes much more taxing when larger intervals are involved. Clef transposition is undoubtedly more accurate, but it does demand of the performer a thorough knowledge of all the clefs.

At first interval transposition may seem easier, but for fluency the authors recommend the use of clefs, especially in those cases where the transposition

v

can be managed by thinking the treble or bass clefs or the more familiar of the C clefs, the alto, tenor, and perhaps the soprano. The mezzo-soprano and baritone clefs are so rarely encountered that few musicians have mastery of them. When these two clefs are needed for transposition it may be simpler to resort to thinking intervals. Yet anyone who has control of the alto, tenor, and soprano clefs can, without undue difficulty, learn the mezzo-soprano and baritone clefs at least well enough to use them for transposition. The student or teacher should choose one method, either intervallic or clef transposition, and use it until the problem is mastered.

To condense even a relatively simple orchestral score at the piano requires considerable pianistic skill, more than many performers on orchestral instruments possess. Yet anyone, despite his technical limitations, can perform on the piano a simple yet faithful version of the score if he can read all of the parts and has learned which ones to simplify or even omit.

The material in this book may be used in the following ways:

1. The students who play piano fluently should play the excerpts as printed.

2. The students who play piano very little may play only one or two of the given parts, while the teacher or other members of the class play the remaining parts.

3. The students who play piano only fairly well may play as many of the parts as they can manage while the teacher or other members of the class play the remaining parts.

After a student has completed this book he should be able, on his own, to develop further his ability to play orchestral scores at the piano by using any of the many scores available, beginning with simpler ones and progressing through those that are more complex.

To develop a skill in score reading the student should have a large amount of material for practice. But the teacher should always be free to use the material in this book in any way he thinks best. If any of the excerpts are too simple, or too difficult, or seem to present no new problems, he may prefer to omit them. Or if he wishes to defer the problem of transposition until the end, he may first use the odd-numbered chapters, then the even-numbered chapters, and close the course with Chapter 13.

Imaginative teachers will find various ways of using the music in this book and should always adapt it to the needs of the students rather than be bound by the organization and procedures the authors have employed.

Robert A. Melcher

Willard F. Warch

TABLE OF TRANSPOSING INSTRUMENTS

INSTRUMENT	KEY	ACTUAL SOUNDS
Piccolos	C	one octave higher
	D-flat	a minor ninth higher
Alto Flute	G	a perfect fourth lower
Oboe d'Amore	A	a minor third lower
English Horn	F	a perfect fifth lower
Clarinets	E-flat	a minor third higher
	D	a major second higher
	C	as written
	B-flat	a major second lower
	A	a minor third lower
Alto Clarinet	E-flat	a major sixth lower
Bass Clarinet	B-flat	a major ninth lower
Contrabassoon		one octave lower
Saxophones		
Soprano	B-flat	a major second lower
Alto	E-flat	a major sixth lower
Tenor	B-flat	a major ninth lower
Baritone	E-flat	an octave and major sixth lower
Bass	B-flat	two octaves and major second lower
Horns*	B-flat (alto)	a major second lower
	A	a minor third lower
	G	a perfect fourth lower
	F	a perfect fifth lower
	E	a minor sixth lower
	E-flat	a major sixth lower
	D	a minor seventh lower
	C	one octave lower
	B-flat basso	a major ninth lower
Trumpets	F	a perfect fourth higher
	E	a major third higher
	E-flat	a minor third higher
	D	a major second higher
	C	as written
	B-flat	a major second lower
	A	a minor third lower
Double Bass		one octave lower

*When low notes for the horns are written on the bass staff, the B-flat basso horn sounds a major second lower than written, the C horn where written, and all the other horns higher than written: the horn in D a major second higher, the horn in E-flat a minor third higher, the horn in E a major third higher, the horn in F a perfect fourth higher, the horn in G a perfect fifth higher, the horn in A a major sixth higher, and the horn in B-flat alto a minor seventh higher. Some twentieth-century composers have tried to correct this illogical procedure by writing notes on the bass staff so that they sound lower than written, just as on the treble staff; in this case, in order to avoid misunderstanding, a footnote is usually given explaining the notation.

NAMES OF ORCHESTRAL INSTRUMENTS

ENGLISH	GERMAN	FRENCH	ITALIAN
Piccolo	*Kleine Flöte*	*Petite Flûte*	*Flauto piccolo, Ottavino*
Flute	*Grosse Flöte*	*Grande Flûte*	*Flauto*
Alto Flute	*Altflöte*	*Flûte en sol*	*Flauto contralto*
Oboe	*Hoboe*	*Hautbois*	*Oboe*
English Horn	*Englisches Horn*	*Cor Anglais*	*Corno inglese*
Clarinet	*Klarinette*	*Clarinette*	*Clarinetto*
Bass Clarinet	*Bassklarinette*	*Clarinette basse*	*Clarinetto basso*
Bassoon	*Fagott*	*Basson*	*Fagotto*
Contrabassoon	*Kontrafagott*	*Contrebasson*	*Contrafagotto*
Saxophone	*Saxophon*	*Saxophone*	*Sassofono*
Horn	*Horn*	*Cor*	*Corno*
Trumpet	*Trompete*	*Trompette*	*Tromba*
Trombone	*Posaune*	*Trombone*	*Trombone*
(Bass) Tuba	*Tuba, Basstuba*	*Tuba (basse)*	*Tuba (bassa)*
Timpani	*Pauken*	*Timbales*	*Timpani*
Bass Drum	*Grosse Trommel*	*Grosse caisse*	*Gran cassa*
Snare Drum	*Kleine Trommel*	*Tambour militaire, caisse*	*Tamburo militare, cassa*
Cymbals	*Becken*	*Cymbales*	*Piatti*
Triangle	*Triangel*	*Triangle*	*Triangolo*
Glockenspiel	*Glockenspiel*	*Glockenspiel, Carillon*	*Campanelli*
Harp	*Harfe*	*Harpe*	*Arpa*
Violin	*Violine, Geige*	*Violon*	*Violino*
Viola	*Bratsche*	*Alto*	*Viola*
Violoncello, Cello	*Violoncell*	*Violoncelle*	*Violoncello*
Double Bass Contra Bass	*Kontrabass*	*Contrabasse*	*Contrabasso*

Chapter 1

THE G AND F CLEFS

In playing three–part open score, it is usually easiest to play the upper two parts with the right hand and the lowest part with the left hand. At times, however, it will be more practical to play only the upper part with the right hand and the lower two parts with the left hand, or even to play all three parts with the right hand. In this and all the following excerpts, each performer should choose the distribution that fits his hands most comfortably and should be free to change this distribution between the two hands at any time he wishes. Bear in mind that at any given moment one of the parts may be the most interesting or thematically important and should be emphasized.

1. Menegali, *Jesu Salvator Mundi*

2. Pisari, O *Salutaris Hostia*

3. Byrd, *Non Nobis, Domine*

When parts for the tenor voice are written on the treble staff, they are sung or played an octave lower than the written pitches.

4. Mozart, *The Magic Flute*, Act II, No. 18,* "O Isis and Osiris!"

*The orchestral parts are omitted.

3

4

5. Palestrina, *Missa Brevis*, "Benedictus II"

In the following excerpt, play the soprano with the right hand, the tenor and bass with the left hand. In measure 3, sustain the G–natural in the soprano with the damper pedal and play the last three notes of the tenor in that measure with the right hand.

6. Haydn, *The Creation*, No. 20, "The Lord is Great"*

*The orchestral parts are omitted.

In four-part music, one usually plays the upper two parts with the right hand and the lower two parts with the left hand. At times, however, it is better to play the upper *three* parts with the right hand, as in measure 4, beat 1, of the following motet.

7. Arcadelt, "Ave Maria"

8. Brahms, *Liebeslieder Walzer*, Op. 52, No. 8*

Im Ländler Tempo

*The piano accompaniment is omitted.

9

9. Schubert, *Der Entfernten*

Tenor I*
Tenor II*
Bass I
Bass II

Langsam

*Note that the two tenor voices are sung or played an octave lower than written.

10

10. Verdi, "Ave Maria"

11. Beethoven, *Mount of Olives, No. 15,* * "Praise our God"

*The orchestral parts are omitted.

12. Handel, *Messiah*, "Behold the Lamb of God"*

*The orchestral parts are omitted.

13. Joseph Wood, "The Lamb" (for mixed chorus)

Allegretto

14. Stravinsky, *Mass for Mixed Chorus and Double Wind Quintet*, "Benedictus" *

*The wind parts are omitted.

In playing music of more than four parts it is impossible to make any detailed suggestions for the distribution of voices in each hand. They must be distributed in whatever way is most pianistically feasible, depending upon the ranges of the individual parts.

15. J. S. Bach, *Cantata No. 27*, Chorale, " Welt, ade! ich bin dein müde"*

*The orchestral parts are omitted.

18

Chapter 2

C, E-FLAT, AND E

INSTRUMENT TRANSPOSITION

C INSTRUMENT TRANSPOSITION

Most orchestral instruments sound the written pitches. This is true for all the strings except the double bass. Basses play from parts written an octave higher than they sound because otherwise there would be many notes written three, four, and five ledger lines below the bass staff; writing the notes up an octave makes them more easily readable.

In addition to the double bass, several other instruments sound an octave lower or higher than their notes are written. The most often encountered are the horn in C, which sounds an octave *lower* than written:

and the piccolo in C, which sounds an octave *higher* than written:

Tchaikovsky, Symphony in F Minor, Op. 36

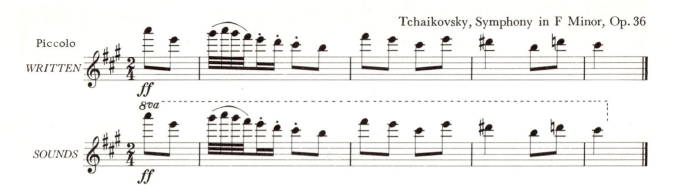

Play the following Mozart Duo as if it were written for horns in C. Remember that the parts sound an octave lower than written.

16. Mozart, Duo for Two Horns, K. 487

Trio

D.C.

E-FLAT INSTRUMENT TRANSPOSITION

For his twelve horn duos Mozart did not specify the keys of the instruments. They could, of course, be played by horns in any key, but Mozart probably intended them for horns in E-flat.

Since E-flat horns sound every note a major sixth lower than written, the first measure of the preceding duo will sound , and so on, throughout the composition.

One can perform this music either by

1. thinking each note down a major sixth in the key of E-flat major or thinking each note up a minor third and playing an octave lower, or

2. substituting the bass clef for the treble clef of the printed score, adding a signature of three flats, and playing an octave higher:

The authors recommend the use of clef transposition because of the wide interval involved in thinking interval-wise and because all musicians are familiar with the bass clef.

There is, however, a problem of accidentals. In measure 13, the printed E-flat on the treble staff for the second horn becomes G-flat on the bass staff, as one would expect. But the printed F-sharp for the first horn becomes A-natural on the bass staff, not A-sharp, because a major sixth below F-sharp is A-natural.

When playing parts for transposing instruments on the piano, observe the following rule to determine which accidentals remain the same and which have to be changed:

Change any accidentals found before the notes that are sharped or flatted in the major scale of the "home key" of the transposing instrument.

21

For example, for an E-flat instrument, B, E, and A on the imagined bass staff become B-flat, E-flat, and A-flat, and any accidentals that appear before these same notes will be *lowered* one half-step. Similarly, for an E instrument, F, C, G, and D on the imagined bass staff become F-sharp, C-sharp, G-sharp, and D-sharp on the imagined bass staff, and any accidentals that appear before those notes will be *raised* one half-step. All other accidentals will remain as printed.

Play the Mozart Duo (No. 16) as if it were for horns in E-flat.
In Number 17, play the horn parts with the left hand and the violin part with the right hand.

17. Haydn, Symphony in E-flat (No. 103)

*Es and Mi♮ are German and Italian respectively for E-flat.

Practice No. 18 in the following ways:

1. Play the horn part while another student plays the string parts.
2. Play the horn, viola, cello, and double bass parts while another plays the first and second violin parts.
3. Play the complete score.

18. Haydn, Symphony in B-flat (No. 51)

The E-flat alto saxophone, like the E-flat horn, sounds a major sixth lower than the printed notes. To transpose the saxophone solo, either think it down a major sixth or imagine the bass staff in the key of A-flat major and play one octave higher; observe the rules for accidentals given on pages 21, 22.

In No. 19 some unessential orchestral parts have been omitted to facilitate performance. In practicing this excerpt, first play the saxophone part alone. Pianists should perform the entire score, playing the violin parts with the right hand and the cello and saxophone parts for the most part with the left hand, arpeggiating the bass where necessary or occasionally playing a cello note an octave higher. Less fluent pianists may play any one part or combination of parts as they can manage.

19. Bizet, *L'Arlésienne* Suite No. 1, "Prelude"

23

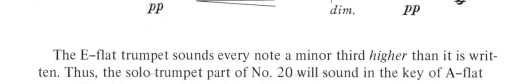

The E-flat trumpet sounds every note a minor third *higher* than it is written. Thus, the solo trumpet part of No. 20 will sound in the key of A-flat major. For this transposition, either think each note up a minor third or imagine the bass clef and play *two* octaves higher.

Observe that in measure 6 of the trumpet part the printed C-sharp becomes E-natural and in measure 7 the printed C-natural becomes E-flat. If using clef transposition, first play the trumpet part by itself as if it were on the bass staff, key of A-flat major, without transposing it up two octaves; then play the trumpet part where it actually sounds.

Less fluent pianists may play only the trumpet part in the proper range while another person plays the accompaniment. More capable pianists should play both the trumpet and piano parts.

20. Haydn, Trumpet Concerto

Horns in E sound a *minor* sixth lower than written. For this transposition, either think every note a minor sixth lower in the key of E major or think each note up a major third and play an octave lower. Or imagine the bass clef in the key of the composition and play an octave higher.

In No. 21 some of the orchestral parts have been omitted. First play the horn parts only. Pianists should then play all the parts. Other students may play any combination of parts they can manage.

21. Mendelssohn, *A Midsummer Night's Dream*, Op. 61, "Nocturne"

26

Chapter 3

THE ALTO CLEF

The alto clef places middle C on the third line, is the "home" clef of the viola, and is sometimes used in writing first and second trombone parts. A clear idea of the pitches represented by this clef can be gained by placing it in reference to the great staff:

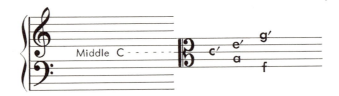

Since the viola is found in nearly every orchestral composition, in most chamber music, and in all string quartets, a knowledge of the alto clef is indispensable to anyone who hopes to become a musician. The alto clef should be as familiar and as easily read as the bass and treble clefs.

If one needs proof of the alto clef's usefulness and suitability to the viola, he should write out the following passage from the viola part of the second movement of the Beethoven String Quartet, Op. 59, No. 3 on either the treble or the bass staff throughout.

Andante con moto quasi Allegretto

The alto clef should be learned "per se," and not by thinking the notes one letter name higher than the treble clef or one letter name lower than the bass clef. This clef will be learned most easily and quickly if the performer will first sing with letter names some melodies written in this clef that can be found in most volumes of sight singing material. Sing the melodies in any convenient octave range; then play them on the piano at the correct pitches.

The viola part of many of the excerpts in this chapter should also be sung in
this fashion before the excerpt is played on the piano.

22. Marcello, Sonata in A Minor

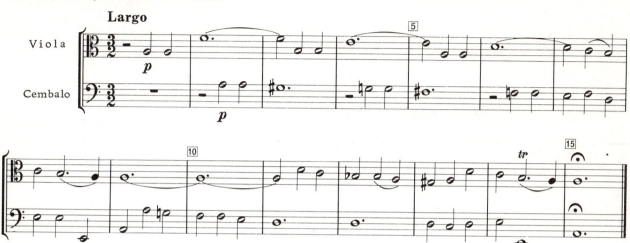

23. Francoeur, Sonata in E Major

24. Marcello, Sonata in F Major

25. J.S. Bach, Choral Prelude, "Ach bleib bei uns, Herr Jesu Christ"

*The pedal part may be played an octave lower than written.

26. Mozart, Duo, K. 424

Andante grazioso

31

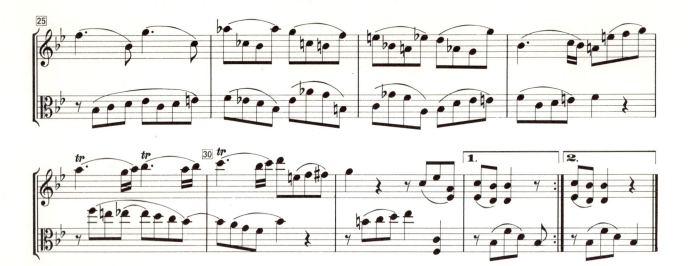

27. Beethoven, Serenade, Op. 25, "Menuetto"

*From here through measure II, play the violin part with the left hand and the viola part with the right hand.

32

28. Mozart, Duo, K. 424

29. Mozart, Duo, K. 423

* From here to the end of this excerpt, play the violin part with the left hand and the viola part with the right hand.

30. Nikos Skalkottas, Duo per Violino e Viola

In the following excerpt, play the viola and cello I parts with the right hand and the cello II and double bass parts *in octaves* with the left hand.

31. Beethoven, Symphony No. 7, Op. 92

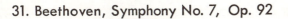

In the following excerpt, play the violin I part with the right hand and the violin II and viola parts with the left hand.

32. Mozart, Symphony in G Minor, K. 550

33. Purcell, *Fantazia No. 3 for Viols*

34. Brahms, Quartet, Op. 60

Observance of the markings R.H. (right hand) and L.H. (left hand) will facilitate the simultaneous performance of all the parts in the following excerpt.

Less skillful pianists may play only one part or combinations of parts as has been suggested in preceding excerpts; they may continue to do so for the rest of the book.

35. Mozart, Divertimento, K. 563, "Menuetto"

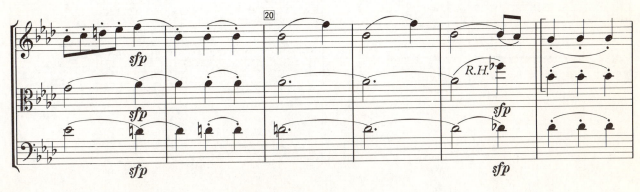

36. Mozart, Divertimento, K. 563

When playing quartets on the piano, the performer may distribute the parts between his two hands in any way that is easiest for him. It may be helpful to mark by brackets the places where part distribution changes.

37. Schubert, String Quartet in D Minor, ("Death and the Maiden")

38. Smetana, String Quartet in E Minor

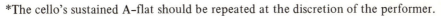

*The cello's sustained A-flat should be repeated at the discretion of the performer.

39. Mozart, Quartet in A Major, K. 464

*Continue this distribution of parts for the first five measures.

Because of excessive spans between parts it is often necessary to make octave adjustments when playing at the piano. In general, it is better to play an inner part or the bass line an octave higher than written; transposing down an octave usually creates a muddy effect. In each case, however, the performer must use his own judgment.

In the following excerpt, between * and *, play the *lower* notes of the violin's double and triple stops an octave higher. Similar adjustments must be made in a few places from measure 25 to the end.

40. Beethoven, Serenade, Op. 25

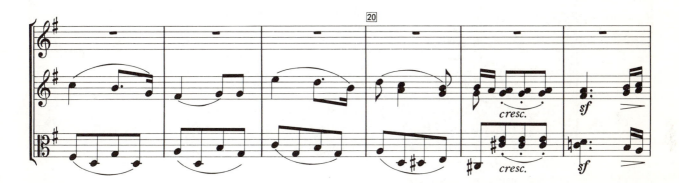

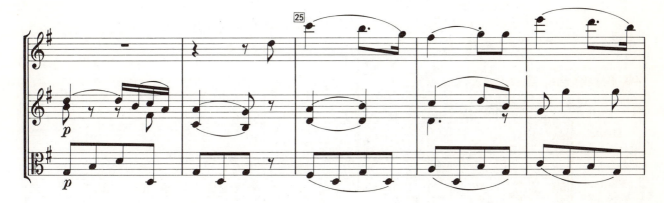

45

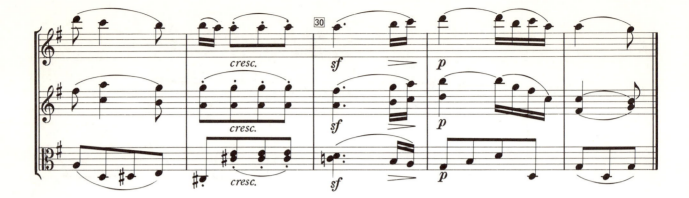

In the following excerpt, at the three places marked *, the viola note may be played an octave higher than written. Measures 39 through 48, first beat, can be played as written, but they will be easier to perform if the cello part is played an octave higher than written.

41. Mozart, Quartet in G Major, K. 387, "Menuetto"

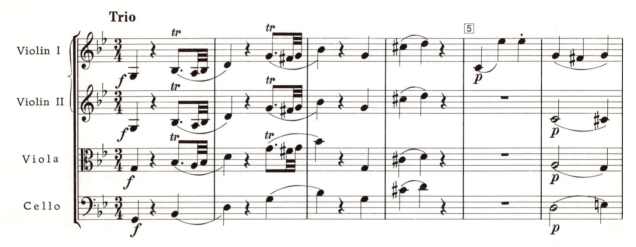

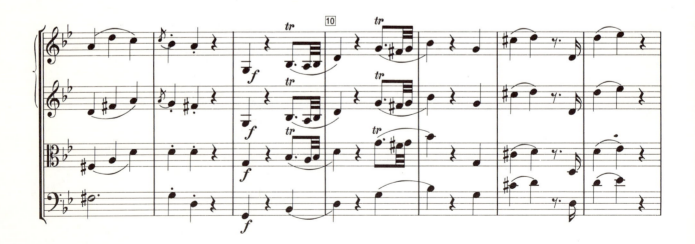

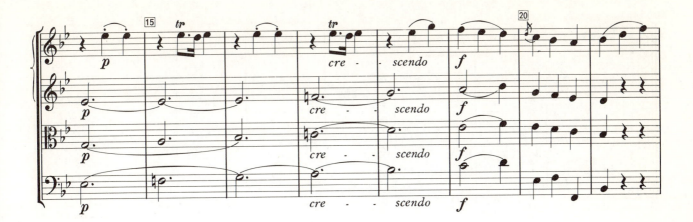

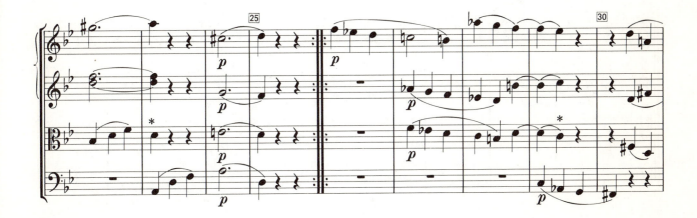

42. Ravel, Ma Mère l'Oye, "Le Jardin Féerique"

43. Elgar, *Enigma Variations (Variations on an Original Theme)*

44. Beethoven, Quartet in C - sharp Minor, Op. 131

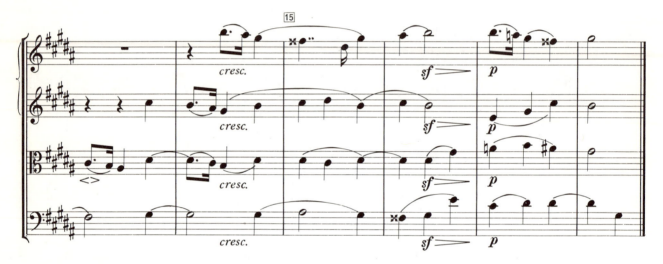

45. Bartok, Fifth Quartet

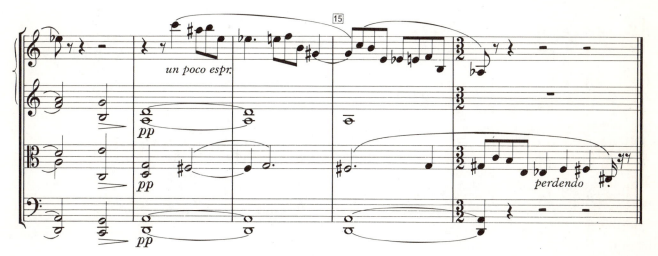

46. Bartók, Sixth Quartet

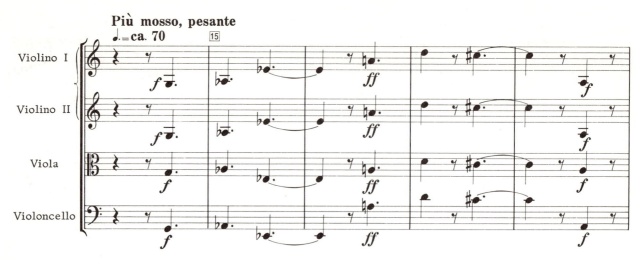

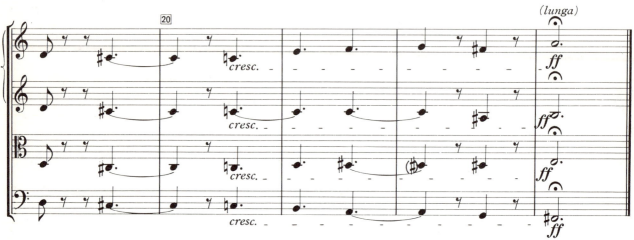

47. Mozart, Quintet in G Minor, K. 516

Chapter 4

D AND D-FLAT
INSTRUMENT TRANSPOSITION

The horn in D sounds all notes a minor seventh lower than they are written. For this transposition either

    1. think each note down a minor seventh, or up a major second and play an octave lower, or

    2. use the alto clef.

Observe that c^2 on the treble staff   becomes d^1 on the alto

staff   Merely think the alto clef with no octave transposition,

in the key in which the composition sounds. F and C on the imagined alto staff become F–sharp and C–sharp.

48. Brahms, Serenade in D Major, Op. 11, "Scherzo"

54

49. Mozart, Horn Concerto in D Major, K. 412

In using clef transposition for D instruments, observe that any accidentals before F and C on the imagined alto staff are raised one half-step. All other accidentals remain as printed.

After having mastered performance of this excerpt, try playing it while looking at the orchestral score. Start at measure 456, first movement.

50. Brahms, Symphony II, Op. 73

51. Rossini, *Semiramide*, Overture

Andantino

Fagotti

Corni in D

The trumpet in D sounds a major second *higher* than written. For this transposition, either think the trumpet part up a major second or use the alto clef in the key of D major and play one octave higher.

52. Purcell, *Dioclesian,* "Trumpet Tune"

53. Purcell, *Birthday Ode for Queen Mary,* "Come Ye Sons of Art"

The E-flat alto saxophone ordinarily sounds a major sixth below the written note; but in the following excerpt, writing the notes a major sixth higher than they sound would require the key of E-sharp minor (8 sharps). For practical reasons Ravel wrote the saxophone part enharmonically in F minor and the transposition is a diminished seventh, playable by thinking the alto clef.

For similar reasons the part of the *corno inglese* (English horn) has been transposed a diminished sixth rather than the customary perfect fifth; therefore, the English horn notes can be read as bass clef up an octave, in the key of G-sharp minor.

54. Moussorgsky - Ravel, *Pictures at an Exhibition,* "The Old Castle"

59

The piccolo in D-flat sounds a minor ninth *higher* than written. Because of the many ledger lines in the following excerpt, it may be easier to think each note up a chromatic half-step and play one octave higher.

If clef transposition is preferred, think the alto clef and play *two* octaves higher. In transposing by clef for a D-flat instrument, the notes B, E, A, D, and G on the imagined alto staff are flatted. Any accidentals appearing before these notes will be lowered one half-step. Accidentals before the other two notes remain as printed.

Performance of this excerpt requires at least two people, one playing the piccolo and trumpet, the other horns and tuba.

55. John Philip Sousa, *The Stars and Stripes Forever*

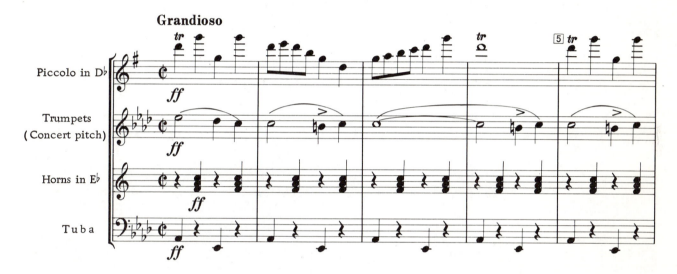

Chapter 5

THE TENOR CLEF

The tenor clef places middle C on the fourth line and is the preferred clef for notation of passages in the middle and upper ranges of the bassoon, the cello, and the trombone. It is also found in some string bass music. Until the mid–nineteenth century vocal music for the tenor voice was written in the tenor clef.

This clef is most clearly understood if seen in its relationship to the great staff:

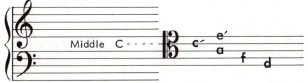

This clef must be practiced until it can be read with ease and fluency if one is to enjoy reading or playing most orchestral scores. Like the alto clef, the tenor and all other C clefs should be learned "per se," and not in relation to the treble or bass clefs. It will be helpful first to sing with letter names melodies on the tenor staff that can be found in most volumes of sight singing material. Many excerpts in this chapter should also be used this way.

56. di Lasso, *Benedictus*

57. J. S. Bach, *Sonata III*

*Suggested performance at the piano:

etc.

58. Tchaikovsky, Symphony IV, Op. 36

In the next three excerpts pianists should play the entire score, cello and piano parts. Less fluent pianists may play the cello part only while another person plays the accompaniment.

59. Dvořák, Cello Concerto in B Minor

60. Brahms, Quartet No. 3 in C Minor, Op. 60

61. Bruch, *Kol Nidrei*, for cello and orchestra

62. Boccherini, Concerto in G Major for Cello and String Orchestra

63. Purcell, *Lord Who Can Tell?*

65. di Lasso, Cantio

66. Purcell, Ode, "Celestial Music"

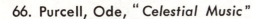

67. Beethoven, *Three Equali for Four Trombones,* No. 3

68. Wagner, *Tristan und Isolde*, "Prelude"

69. Brahms, Piano Quartet No. 1 in G Minor, Op. 25, "Finale"

*This cadenza-like passage is generally begun in a moderate tempo, which is then gradually speeded up to a true *presto* at the point where the piano enters.

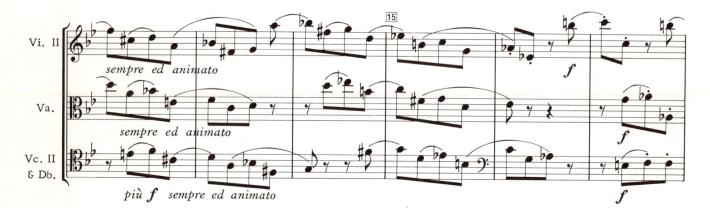

70. Mozart, Quartet, K. 589

71. Brahms, Symphony III, Op. 90*

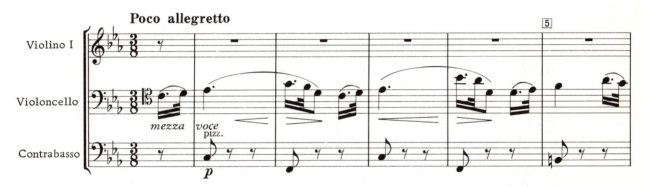

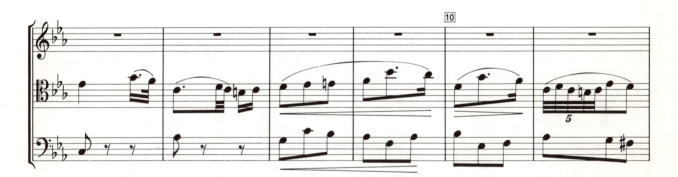

*The accompanying instruments are omitted in this excerpt.

72. Brahms, Symphony II, Op. 73 *

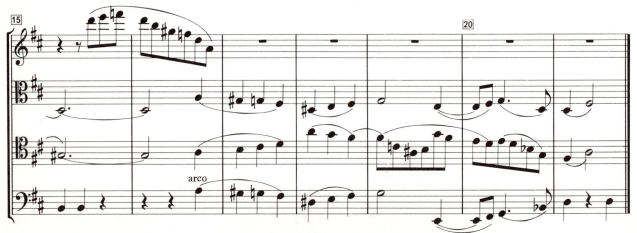

*The accompanying instruments are omitted in this excerpt.

73. J. S. Bach, Suite VI for Unaccompanied Cello, "Sarabande"*

*In the manuscript by Anna Magdalena Bach, which is the most authentic version, this music appears in an alternation of alto and bass clefs, but modern editions use the tenor and bass clefs. This excerpt contains all the notes and phrasings as they appear in the manuscript, although the more recent usage of the tenor and bass clefs has been employed.

74. Tchaikovsky, *Variations on a Rococo Theme*

In condensing the following excerpt on the piano, tap the introductory drum solo with the left hand on the piano case; play the bassoon parts with the right hand and only the double bass (or double bass and cello) with the left hand. Adding any of the other string notes will obscure the bassoon duet and even falsify its rhythmic effect (e.g., measure 12).

75. Bartók, Concerto for Orchestra, Second Movement ("Giuoco delle Coppie")

Chapter 6

B-FLAT INSTRUMENT TRANSPOSITION

The horn in B–flat basso sounds all notes a major ninth lower than they are written. For this transposition either

    1. think each note down a major ninth, or down a major second and play an octave lower, or

    2. use the tenor clef.

Observe that c^2 on the treble staff   becomes b

or, with an appropriate signature, b–flat   on the tenor staff.

Merely think the tenor clef with no octave transposition, in the key in which the composition sounds.

In transposing for any B–flat instrument, the notes B and E on the imagined tenor staff become B-flat and E-flat. Any accidentals appearing before B and E will be lowered one half-step. All other accidentals remain as printed.

Play No. 76 as if it were for two horns in B–flat basso.

76. Mozart, Duo for Two Horns, K. 487

The following instruments

> clarinet in B-flat (soprano),
> trumpet and cornet in B-flat,
> horn in B-flat alto

sound all notes a major second lower than they are written. To transpose music for these instruments, either think each note down a whole–step or use the tenor clef and play an octave higher in the appropriate key.

Return to the preceding excerpt and play it as if it were for two horns in B–flat alto.

77. Beethoven, Trio, Op. 11

*In German editions of music B-flat is called B, and B-natural is called H.

78. Beethoven, Trio, Op. 11

79. Beethoven, Duo for Clarinet and Bassoon

80. Bizet, Carmen, Act I, "Entracte"

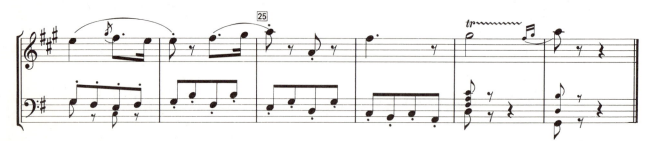

*The other orchestral parts are omitted here.

81. Haydn, Symphony in E-flat (No. 103)

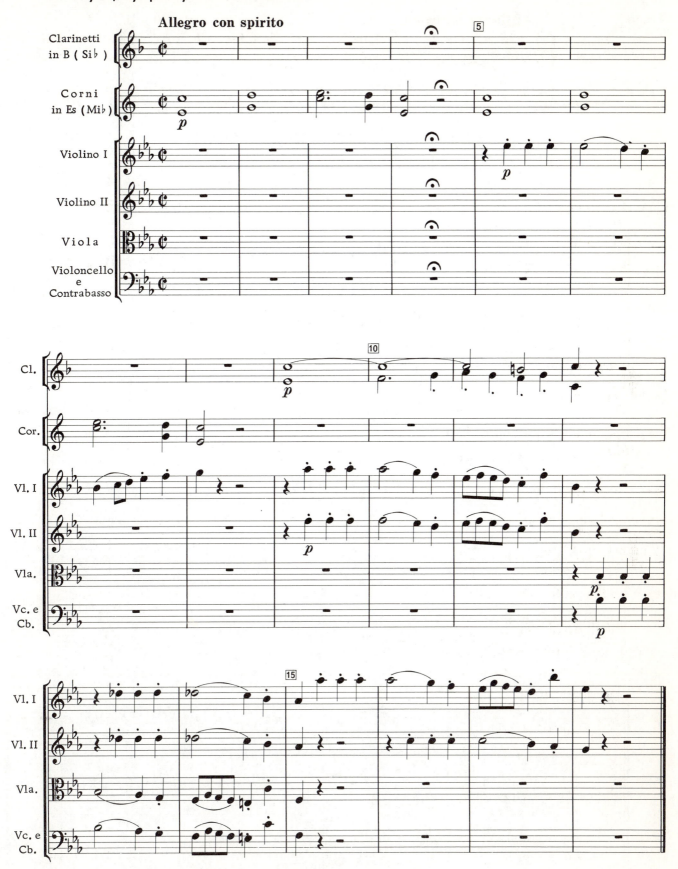

82. Brahms, Serenade in D Major, Op. 11, "Minuet"

Klarinette I in B
Klarinette II in B
Fagott I

piano e dolce
p

5

10

83. Mozart, Serenade, K.375

Menuetto

Corni I, II in E♭
Clarinetti I, II in B♭
Fagotti I, II

p
p
5
p cresc.
p cresc.

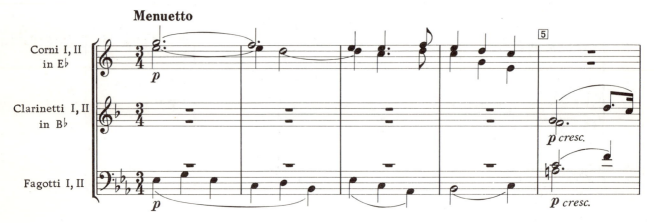

p
cresc.
p
p
cresc.
p

The following excerpt is most easily performed by two pianists, one playing the woodwind parts, the other the string parts. When one person plays the entire score he will have to make certain adjustments, as at measure 4, where he must either omit the first beat of the woodwinds and play the entire string passage, or resolve the woodwinds on the first beat and begin the string parts on the second beat. Measure 5, first beat, should be played from the woodwind parts and the string parts ignored. Similar procedures must be followed throughout this excerpt.

84. Brahms, Symphony III, Op. 90

90

86. R. Strauss, Serenade, Op. 7

91

87. R. Strauss, Serenade, Op. 7

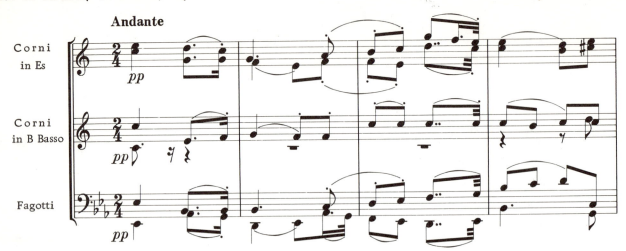

Chapter 7

THE SOPRANO CLEF

The soprano clef was widely used in keyboard music and music for women's voices until the nineteenth century and was used to some extent for vocal music down to the twentieth century.

One cannot read music contained in the authoritative complete editions of such composers as Bach, Mozart, Haydn, or Mendelssohn, or other collections of Renaissance and Baroque music, without a knowledge of this clef.

It places middle C on the first line of the staff and is related to the treble staff as follows:

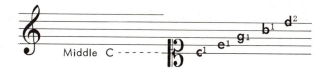

Like the alto and tenor clefs, the soprano clef should be learned "per se," and not in relation to other clefs. It will be helpful to sing with letter names melodies on the soprano staff that can be found in volumes of sight singing material. Many excerpts from this chapter should also be used this way.

88. J. S. Bach, *Little Notebook for Anna Magdalena Bach*

89. J. S. Bach, *St. Matthew Passion*, "Ich will dir mein Herze schenken"

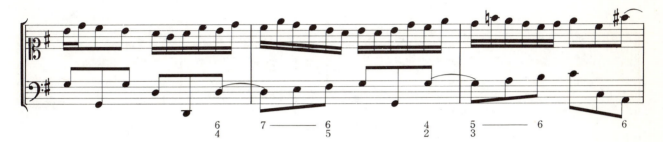

90. J. S. Bach, *Little Notebook for Anna Magdalena Bach*

Polonaise.

91. J. S. Bach, *Little Notebook for Anna Magdalena Bach*

92. Mendelssohn, *Elijah,* "Lord, Bow Thine Ear"

93. Mozart, *Notturno,* K. 436, "Ecco quel Fiero Istante"*

*The accompaniment of three basset horns is omitted.

D.C. al ⊕

94. Lotti, *Vere Languores Nostros*

95. Mendelssohn, *Elijah,* "Lift Thine Eyes"

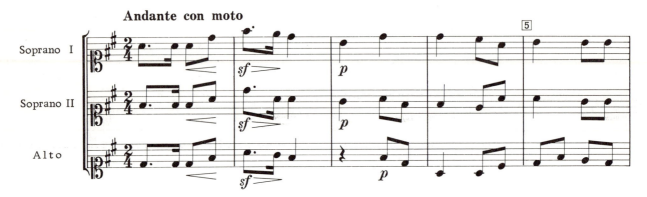

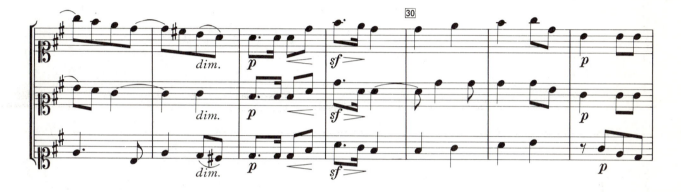

96. Mendelssohn, *Elijah*, "Baal, we Cry to Thee"

97. Palestrina, *Jesu, Rex Admirabilis*

98. Purcell, Fantazia No.12 for Viols

99. di Lasso, *Matona, mia cara*

Chapter 8

A AND A-FLAT
INSTRUMENT TRANSPOSITION

The horn in A, trumpet in A, clarinet in A, and oboe d'amore sound all notes a *minor* third lower than they are written. For this transposition either

    1. think each note down a minor third, or

    2. use the soprano clef.

Observe that c^2 on the treble staff 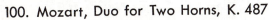 becomes a^1 on the

soprano staff 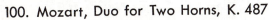 . In transposing for any instrument in A, the notes F, C, and G on the imagined soprano staff become F-sharp, C-sharp, and G-sharp. Any accidentals appearing before F, C, or G will be raised one half-step. All other accidentals remain as printed.

Play the following excerpt as if for two horns in A.

100. Mozart, Duo for Two Horns, K. 487

101. Enesco, Roumanian Rhapsody No. 1, Op. 11

102. J.S. Bach, Cantata No. 136, *Es kommt ein Tag*

Oboe d'Amore in A

Continuo

In the following excerpt Verdi asks for long ceremonial trumpets in A-flat. To transpose music for an A-flat instrument, either think each note down a *major* third or use the soprano clef. Observe that the notes B, E, A, and D on the imagined soprano staff become B-flat, E-flat, A-flat, and D-flat. Any accidentals appearing before B, E, A, or D will be lowered one half-step. All other accidentals remain as printed.

103. Verdi, *Aida*, Act II, "Triumphal March"

104. Brahms, Quintet in B Minor, Op. 115 *

*Violins I and II are tacet during this passage.
†Arpeggiate the first bass note and play the first three notes of the cello part an octave higher, thus:

105. Weber, Oberon, "Overture"

109

106. Mozart, Quintet, K. 581, "Minuet"

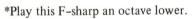

*Play this F-sharp an octave lower.

107. Tchaikovsky, Ouverture-Fantaisie, Francesca da Rimini

Andante cantabile non troppo

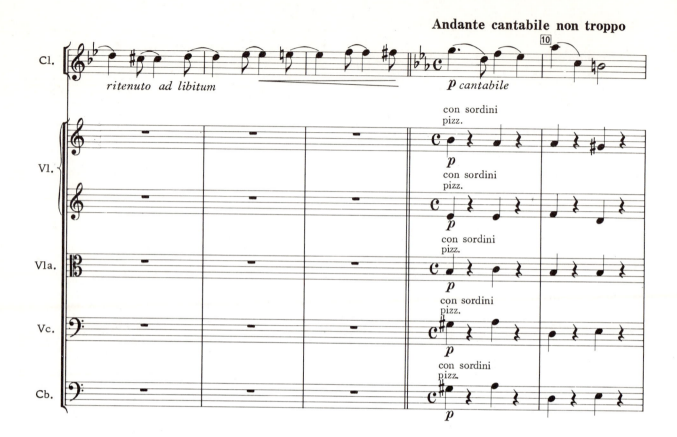

108. Schubert, Symphony in B Minor

113

109. Mendelssohn, Violin Concerto in E Minor, Op. 64

110. Stravinsky, Octet for Wind Instruments*

*The other instruments are tacet during this passage.

If the following excerpt is played by two people, one playing the clarinet part and the other the string accompaniment, the person playing the string parts can play every note as written if he will play the cello with the left hand and violins and viola with the right hand, except in measures 12, 14, 15, 17, and 18, where the left hand will play cello and viola.

However, if the excerpt is played by one performer, it will be best for him to play only the clarinet melody with the right hand. The left hand can play the bass notes and the proper chords, keeping to the actual notes of the first violin as much as possible and making whatever adjustments are necessary in the second violin and viola parts. Start:

Larghetto

111. Mozart, Quintet, K, 581

Larghetto

Chapter 9

THE MEZZO-SOPRANO CLEF

The mezzo–soprano clef places middle C on the second line

It was used for both vocal and instrumental music until about the eighteenth century. Although it is encountered in the scholarly editions of Medieval and Renaissance music, perhaps its chief use today is in transposing music written for instruments in F. It is related to the great staff as follows:

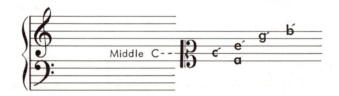

To facilitate learning this clef, first sing the mezzo–soprano clef parts of the following excerpts with pitch names.

112. di Lasso, *Missa ad Imitationen Moduli Iager, "Benedictus"*

113. di Lasso, *Expandi Manus Meas*

119

114. Ingegneri, *Inter Iniquos*

115. Ingegneri, *Cumque Injecissent Manus*

116. Byrd, *Mass for Three Voices,* "Kyrie"

117. Purcell, *My Song Shall Be Alway*

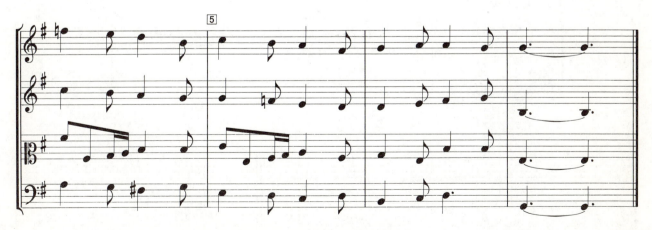

*Purcell used the mezzo-soprano clef for the viola part.

Chapter 10

F INSTRUMENT TRANSPOSITION

The horn in F and the English horn (an alto oboe in F) sound all notes a perfect fifth lower than they are written. For this transposition either

    1. think each note down a perfect fifth, or

    2. use the mezzo-soprano clef.

Observe that c^2 on the treble staff becomes f^1 on the

mezzo–soprano staff . In transposing for any F instrument, the

note B on the imagined mezzo–soprano staff becomes B–flat. Any accidentals appearing before B will be lowered one half–step. All other accidentals remain as printed.

Play the following excerpt as if for two horns in F.

118. Mozart, Duo for Two Horns, K. 487

122

Trio

*For horn notation on the bass staff, see footnote to *Table of Transposing Instruments,* page vii .

119. J. S. Bach, Brandenburg Concerto No. 1*

Corno I in F

Corno II in F

120. J. S. Bach, Brandenburg Concert No. 1 *

Corni I in F II

Continuo

*The other instruments are omitted in this excerpt.

121. Beethoven, Trio, Op. 87

Oboe I

Oboe II

Englisches Horn

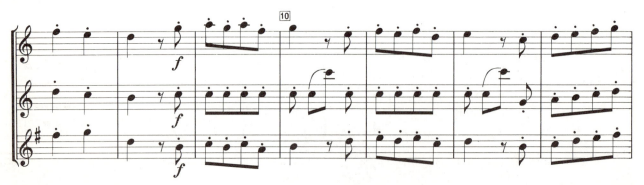

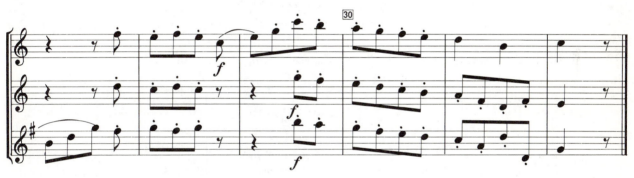

122. Beethoven, Trio, Op. 87

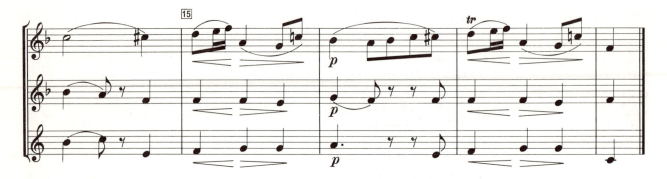

123. J. S. Bach, *Christmas Oratorio,* "*Fallt mit Danken, Fallt mit Loben*" *

*The other instruments are omitted in this excerpt.

†When playing all parts together, the second and third notes of this measure may be played an octave higher.

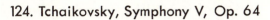

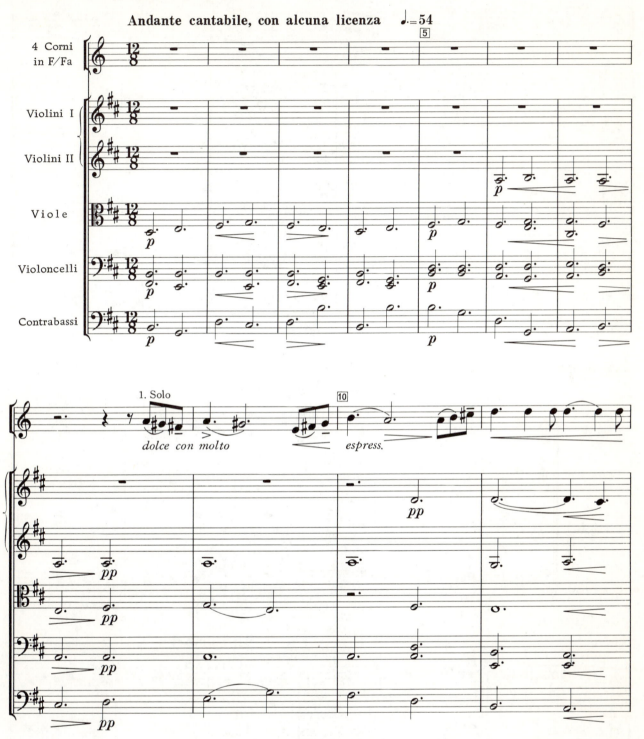

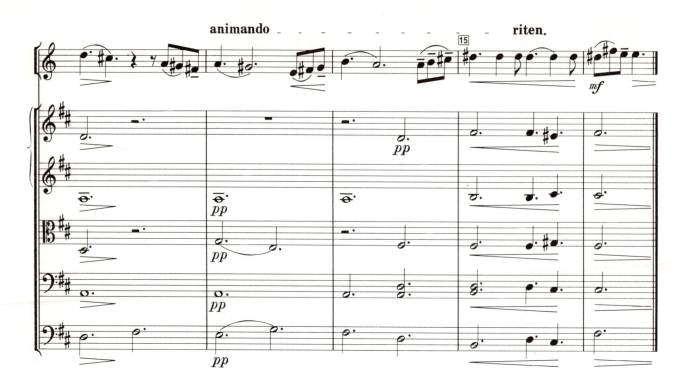

125. Schubert, Octett, Op. 166*

*Violins I and II and viola are omitted in this excerpt.

126. Tchaikovsky, Ouverture-Fantaisie, *Romeo et Juliette**

*The viola and bassoon parts are omitted; they duplicate the English horn and cello respectively. All other instruments are tacet during this passage.

127. Rimsky-Korsakoff, *Capriccio Espagnol**

*When playing all parts together, play the upper three horns with the right hand and the fourth horn and strings with the left hand. Or the fourth horn may be omitted since it is essentially duplicated by the viola.

128. Strauss, *Till Eulenspiegels lustige Streiche, Op. 28**

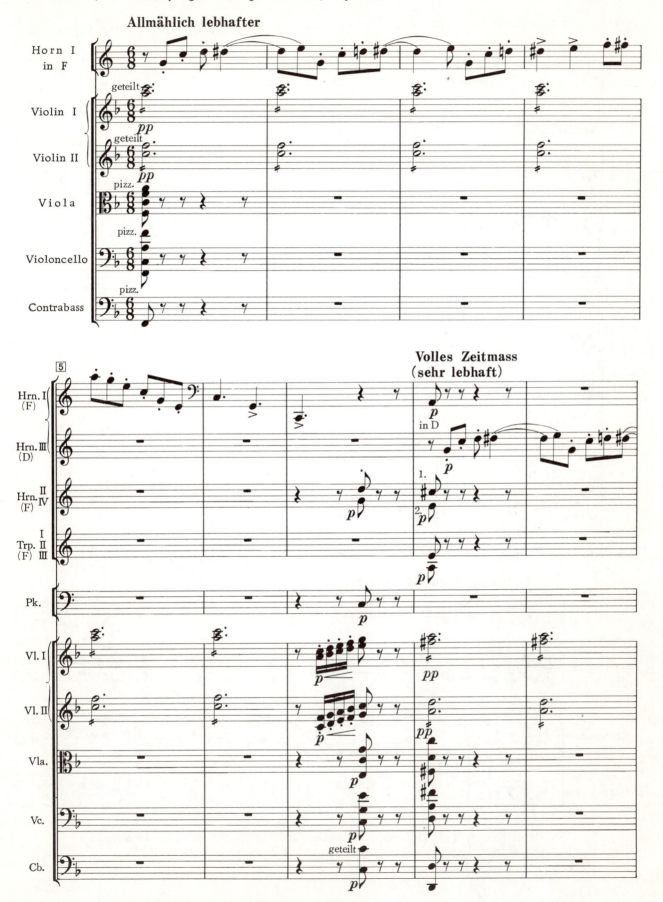

*The woodwinds are omitted in this passage.

129. Beethoven, Symphony VIII, Op. 93*

*When playing all parts together, in measures 1 and 3 of the cello part play the second, third, and fourth notes an octave lower; in measures 5 through 7 play the second horn part an octave higher.

132

130. Britten, *The Young Person's Guide to the Orchestra*, Op. 34

*The trumpet in C is non-transposing.

131. Wagner, *Siegfried Idyll*

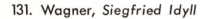

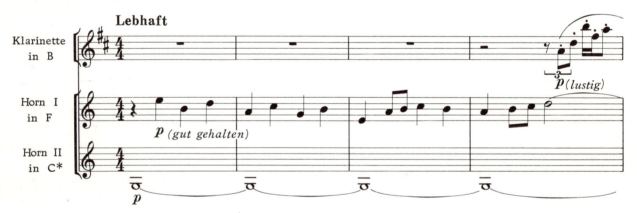

*The horn in C sounds an octave lower than written.

* Suggested performance of the last measure:

132. Humperdinck, *Hänsel und Gretel*, "Vorspiel"

*Play this note an octave higher or as a grace note before the horns.

133. von Weber, Der Freischütz, "Overture"*

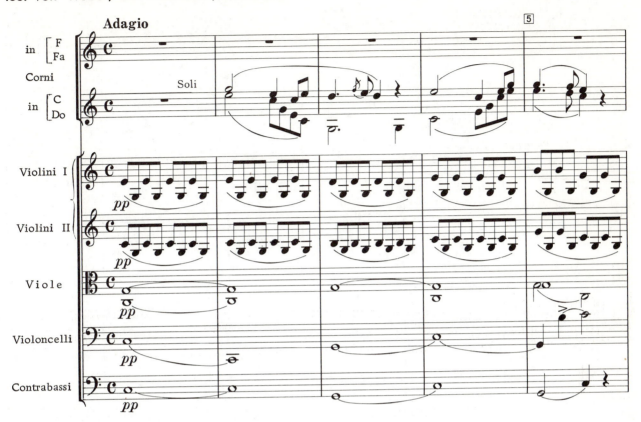

*This excerpt can be performed by two people, one playing the horn parts and the other the strings. If it is performed by one person, he should concentrate on the melody, bass, correct chords, and keeping the rhythm going in its steady eighth-note pattern without worrying about each and every note of the accompaniment. Begin:

The trumpet in F sounds all notes a perfect fourth higher than written. To transpose music for this instrument, either think the mezzo–soprano clef up an octave or play each note up a perfect fourth.

134. J. S. Bach, Brandenburg Concert No. 2

The following excerpt can be performed by three people, one playing the trumpet parts, another the first harp and timpani parts, and the third the remaining parts. Or two people can divide the parts, one doing the trumpets and double basses, the other the remaining parts. (Ignore the second harp, since it only doubles notes already present in other parts.)

If one performer attempts the entire score, he will have to play with his left hand the double bass on the beat and the first cello on the after beat, and with his right hand the trumpets plus those of the first harp notes that are necessary to complete the harmony.

135. Debussy, *Fêtes*

Chapter 11

THE BARITONE CLEF

The baritone clef places the F below middle C on the third line:

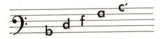

Theoretically, this clef may also be represented by middle C on the fifth line:

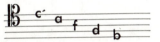

It was used in earlier centuries and is still encountered in some scholarly editions of Medieval and Renaissance music. However, its most practical use today is in transposing music for instruments in G.

To facilitate learning this clef, first sing with letter names the baritone clef parts of the following excerpts.

136. di Lasso, *Justus Cor Suum*

137. Byrd, Mass for Three Voices, "Agnus Dei"

138. Byrd, Mass for Four Voices, "Gloria"

139. Ingegneri, *Insurrexerunt*

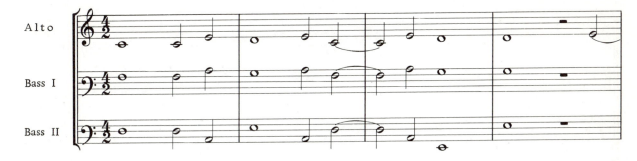

140. Byrd, Mass for Four Voices, "Agnus Dei"

Soprano

Tenor

Bass

Chapter 12

G INSTRUMENT TRANSPOSITION

The horn in G and the alto flute both sound all notes a perfect fourth lower than they are written. For this transposition either

    1. think each note down a perfect fourth, or

    2. use the baritone clef and play one octave higher.

Observe that c^2 on the treble staff becomes small g on the

baritone staff . The note F on the imagined baritone staff becomes F-sharp. Any accidental appearing before F will be raised one half-step. All other accidentals remain as printed.

Play the following excerpt as if for two horns in G.

141. Mozart, Duo for Two Horns, K. 487

142. Bach, Cantata No. 79, Gott, der Herr, ist Sonn und Schild *

*The other parts are omitted in this excerpt.

143. J. S. Bach, Cantata No. 100, *Was Gott thut, das ist wohlgethan**

*The other parts are omitted in this excerpt.

144. Handel, *Judas Maccabeus,* **"Chorus of Youths"**

145. Haydn, Symphony No. 54 in G Major

146. Mozart, Symphony No. 40 in G Minor, K. 550, "Minuet, Trio"

153

147. Holst, *The Planets*, "Neptune, the Mystic"*

Copyright in U.S.A. 1921 by Goodwin and Tabb, Ltd. Used by permission.

*The other instruments are tacet during this excerpt.
†The alto flute in G is sometimes erroneously called the bass flute.
††Suggested performance for the harp tremolo:

155

Chapter 13

THE FULL SCORE *

It is obviously impossible to play all the notes of an orchestral score on the piano. Some parts will have to be condensed, simplified, or omitted entirely. The important thing is to *read* all of the parts, to play as many as practical, and to come as close as possible to the composer's intentions. The following principles should be of help:

1. Play the melody as written, though it may be necessary at times to transpose it up or down an octave. The melody may, of course, be found in any instrument but most frequently in the first violin.
2. Play the bass line (most often found in the cello, double bass, bassoon, and tuba) as written, transposing it up an octave when necessary.
3. Read the harmonies of the inner parts carefully, distributing the chords between the two hands as feasible. Often these parts cannot be played where written. In general, it is better to transpose them up rather than down in order to avoid "muddiness."
4. Note the duplication of parts and play them as one line.
5. Counter melodies, subsidiary lines, and filigree parts will often have to be omitted.
6. The rhythmic patterns of accompaniment parts will often have to be simplified. Try to maintain their character as closely as is pianistically possible. Fast repeated notes, easy to play on an orchestral instrument but often clumsy on the piano, are best changed into a broken pattern or tremolo. See excerpts Nos. 149 (measures 5–12), 156, and 157.

How much of the score the performer can reproduce on the piano will, of course, depend upon his piano technique. But even a person lacking fluency can manage a simple reduction if he has carefully read all of the parts. No. 148 shows a full score in a transcription suitable for a fairly skilled pianist and another reduction as it might be played by a pianist of limited technique. In the simpler version, note that the bass has been raised an octave and that many doublings, especially the lower octave of the melody, have been omitted to facilitate performance. No. 149 shows one practical reduction of part of Beethoven's Egmont Overture; this can be further simplified if necessary.

After carefully studying these excerpts, apply the principles observed to the remaining excerpts.

*For a more detailed discussion of playing full scores on the piano, see Eric Taylor, *Playing from an Orchestral Score* (New York: Oxford University Press, Inc., 1967), Introduction.

149. Beethoven, *Egmont Overture*, Op. 84

159

160

162

151. Haydn, Symphony in D Major ("London" set No. 2)

153. Schumann, Symphony I, Op. 38

At first glance the following two excerpts seem to pose problems of transposition and simultaneous thinking of several different clefs. However, a little
study reveals many duplications of parts. Such doublings, frequently encountered in orchestral scores, allow one to play the part from the most easily
read clef.

154. Bizet, *Carmen*, "Prelude"

171

155. Dvořák, Symphony No. 8 in G Major, Op. 88

172

173

In the following three excerpts simple realizations of the accompaniment patterns are given. Continue the reductions in the styles suggested.

156. Beethoven, *Prometheus* Overture, Op. 43

157. Mozart, Symphony No. 40 in G Minor, K. 550

158. Berlioz, *Harold in Italy*, Op. 16

It is practically impossible to play on the piano all the notes of this final excerpt. Below it is given the first two measures of the piano solo as Ravel composed it before arranging it for orchestra. Below that is an even simpler reduction. Continue the reduction in whichever style is feasible.

159. Ravel, *Pavane pour une infante défunte*